INFREQUENT MYSTERIES

poems by
Pamela Stewart

INFREQUENT MYSTERIES

alicejamesbooks
Cambridge, Massachusetts

Grateful acknowledgment is made to the following magazines in which a number of these poems, some in earlier versions, first appeared: (U.S.A.) *The American Poetry Review:* "Sunbathing"; *Columbia:* "Something, which waits,..."; *Crazyhorse:* "The Crickets of Amherst" and "Naive Reading"; *High Plains Literary Review:* "The Edge of Things," "Infrequent Mysteries" (except section 6) and "Modesty"; *raccoon:* "The Elvis Wall" and "Good Friday." (U.K.) *The New Welsh Review:* "Lesson of the Day"; *Oxford Magazine:* "The Canoe in the Forest," "Our Solitudes" and "Wrong Weather"; *Planet:* "Fiction's Daughter" and "Dogs"; *Poetry Durham:* "To S. Kazuko"; *Poetry Wales:* "Figure & Ground" and "On Translation"; *Writing Women:* "Domestics"; *Westwords:* "Melancholia."

"Promises," "Lesson of the Day," "Domestics," "Fiction's Daughter," "The Question of Noon," "Dogs," and "On a Drab December Hill" also appeared in *Peterloo Preview 2*, Peterloo Poets, Calstock, Cornwall, U.K. 1990. "Autumn is a Place" appeared in *Poetry Matters*, 1990, Peterloo Poets.

Cover and text design by Charles Casey Martin.
Cover photograph by E. J. Cothey.
Printed by Evans Printing Company, Concord, New Hampshire.
Epigraph © 1987, Bloodaxe Books
from Tomas Tranströmer's *Collected Poems*
translated by Robin Fulton.

Alice James Books gratefully acknowledges support from the National Endowment for the Arts and from the Massachusetts Council on the Arts and Humanities, a state agency whose funds are recommended by the Governor and appropriated by the State Legislature.

Alice James Books are published by the Alice James Poetry Cooperative, Inc.
Alice James Books, 33 Richdale Ave., Cambridge, MA 02140

for E.J.

CONTENTS

ONE

TWO

THREE

Notes

*It hurts to go through walls, it makes you ill
but it is necessary.
The world is one. But walls . . .
And the wall is part of yourself—
we know or we don't know, . . .*

*The clear sky has leant itself against the wall.
It's like a prayer to the emptiness.
And the emptiness turns its face to us
and whispers
'I am not empty, I am open.'*

— Tomas Tranströmer

ONE

THE BOSTONIAN READING AMICHAI

In our house, no one was taught
to argue with God. So how could I
disbelieve my nightlight, resist
my pink-and-blue picture books,
or the dove on top of the Christmas tree?
All the glistening meats and cakes
might vaporize, and bedtime stories

unwrite themselves, give over
to bad dreams. I never knew
there was a tradition of despair
in other households, or any need
for salvation. Nothing exact
ever called to me. Even now,
bewildered by the state of the world,

of my life, I don't rage
as other women do. Neither
do I have their faith. I don't argue
with God how none of it makes sense.
That's simply how it is—
like the original blur at the edge of light
the nightlight cast.

SUNBATHING

Here, buttercups extend their hard luster
beneath the sky. They gleam
beside a boulder where crows gather
to decide on flight. Buttercups
insist on yellow in this tall,
tangled grass which enfolds the hill
in that jewel-deep green
which will no longer exist when heat
goes solid in June. This hill
is a headland struck stubborn against the sea.

Today, women in striped skirts and summer blouses,
husbands with loosened collars, stroll
unpinning their faces into the sun.
Dogs ruffle among frail, sugar-pink campion,
mop-nosed thrift, and my brash
resilient buttercups. A wavering sweetness
chimes from these tourist voices
as they call one another to shelter from wind.

Who, this moment, could believe that the silver-
blue water—spread so far the world's curve
shows—is slamming at sand, rock, iron
and bone beneath its glittery skin? Who'd dare
believe that sun won't shine forever
or that these flowers, tilting just so,
could ever be annulled? This hour in May
sweeps toward a summit of sky
before hunger sets in and the rash
of too much light prickles the skin.

The buttercup nearest my eye
has a circular puncture where an insect has been.
I don't touch that petal,
but lean into its hard yellow shine

through which I see an emerald speck of grass
then such busy darkness
the trembling begins.

REMISSION

In the tall russet-flecked trees of autumn
some bird coughs repeatedly. The thunk
of an ax from a distant hill
sends rooks screeching like warning. Slowly,
a man walks with that cadence
which lifts one foot, then the other,
to punctuate present from past.
What he's not, who he's not, clicks
into this figure on a path
which will return to the exact door
closed just minutes ago.

In this damp air, the thin skin of his wrists
shines. Breeze slicks through his hair.
Before long his bones will break
their disguise and drift out to sea.
His blood knows this, knows how first
he learned to hide away the feathers, pebbles,
and treasured words of childhood
in pockets and drawers. Then he learned
to hide himself. Now all we see
is someone in a forest scuffing leaves
against freshening wind.

MY NEIGHBOR AND MYSELF

When I was seven I used to kneel
on the twilit lawn and speak to God
as he stretched awake in our vast
maple tree while night eased down
on Brookline, Massachusetts.
Across the street the grubby Mercer kids,
who always stayed up late, stood
on their porch and laughed at me.
What hurt started to rebuild my face
from outside-in as I strolled away
towards book, rabbit, and bear.

One day Susie Mercer stepped out
of her doorway in a white frilled dress.
Flowers in her hair floated their halo
of scent above freckles and a well-
scrubbed neck. Surprised, I told her
she was pretty. Her mother swept up
saying it was Susie's First Communion
then trooped the whole shining family
down the street. I sat on the stoop,
watching, and thought how God receives us
both all dressed up, or huddled
in pajama dark. Perhaps Susie Mercer

now maneuvers a raft of kids
back and forth to school, keeps
a rosary in her bedside drawer. I hadn't
said her name out loud in years
until last night: giddy and rude,
I'd laughed at someone who was serious.
The sound, sharpened by age but not
deliberate, snapped me back to my own
small heart drumming with rage
on porch-lit summer nights. I'd been so sure

I'd got it right about trees and stars
and God. But a bright hem swinging
above polished shoes, a string
of funny beads, infected me with doubt
that there was only one
proper way to say a prayer, or
I'm sorry to a reticent white face
clenching its hammer and nails
above the dinner table.

OCCULTATIONS

A few streets away, there's a wall
hung with paintings of torsos and legs.
It's important to stare, as the artist did,
directly between those legs
into the very wide, wing-flat centers
which are emphatically dark
but cannot be entered.
                        Clearly,

the black black paint is spread
as on a mirror where finger and eye
must scrape past mystery
toward resemblance.
                      This is one story

of dying and why I must speak
of the dream I lived last night. My father,
in loose trousers and jacket, had wild
white hair in the wind. Drunk,
he walked the ledges of high buildings
above a courtyard where a crowd watched.
He poised his arms for flight
down into the dark their faces made while I,
who wore no daughter's face, wouldn't follow
to keep the old man from falling.
                      It's important

that the ledges of those buildings
were as Mediterranean-white
as that wall of torsos and legs
where the observed textures and tones
of woman hold our attention.
                      There,

everything's exact, even the opaque
black mysteries
where another man flew into his face
before painting it out.

THEIR HOUSE

Her window opens to twilight. The basin
by the sill also holds twilight while her face
glows whiter than the sky. Water
skims her hands, forehead, shoulders.
One old sugar maple is a giant on the lawn
though the house gets smaller every year.

At window's edge, dusk
hovers longer than in cities, or on the sea.
Hurt was possible to lose
within the orchard, by the stream—no matter
voices slamming about the rooms, no matter
the unattended kettle hissing.

Now she trusts those voices are in heaven,
or down the well covered by stone.
They can't get out,
or turn on her from across the world.
Her mouth begins a sound.

THE EDGE OF THINGS

You want to know who sleeps on the other side
of the wall—there's a feeling
of needles in his legs, a silence of orphans.

His name and age are not important. He must
be less than young. Over that tree,
a hawk blesses one of his hands.
You are not sure, right or left. Or do they mean
the print of ash across his mouth?

Sudden blue shadows fall. Lanterns
cross then uncross on water below white
fingers of fog. You recognize
the prisoner's mirror webbing ice to stone.

One side of the wall is unbearable softness.

A red star twists down into the lake.
He turns over, recalls
the single bright blossom of a geranium.
You recall it dropping to the sill, then down
between the cat's paws. It is all
black and white, except for what falls.

The candle in the coffin by the water goes out.

You want to know why this someone is sleeping
during the exact moments that you sleep.
Does he pity you? Who
is so insistent at the door—and whose
house is it anyway?

ON REREADING, YET AGAIN,
TENDER IS THE NIGHT

I must never fill my glass
with wine from Italy
or France. I might crack bone
on rock again, or stand
like Dr. Diver by the phone
not as good
as I'd intended to be.
I must slam shut my mouth
on ungiven kisses
though my ribs
splay from the density.
The mind gets drunk enough
by candlelight
for no good reason
but a few words splashing in air
above the white
flicker of a wrist.
Later, my legs kick
beneath covers. Illicit dreams
spatter my sleep. I pull
my pillow against me
as Mr. Moon
drenches the bed with his chilled
gin-blue. Dick Diver
soothes Nicole, hangs up
the phone in a haze
of betrayal. I shudder awake
at light's unbidden
parting of drapes.
Back at the bar,
Dick Diver hunches his face into
my other life.

LESSON OF THE DAY

Curled against my pillows in a castle
in Scotland, I read about a lady
who makes me wince to be American.
All that money, parties, that daft chase
after Royalty's attention. Imagine—
spraying curtains with ground glass,
or draping rooms so thick with roses
guests sickened from the scent. Diamonds,
silks, mink. And such vanity!

Laura's wigwam they called that case
full of secret hair: dishevelled
to wake up in, or a windswept wig
for country walks, tight shining curls
for evening wear. All brunette
so her blonde impoverished childhood
was tucked away the day she married money.
But Mrs. Corrigan,

I read on, begin to like you and wonder,
when you were Laura Mae
helping your Ma cook for lumberjacks,
did hot fat splash up and your hair
never grow back? Maybe
when God whispered in a dream "If you
stand on your head each day
I'll make you rich" you scraped
against a nail in the backyard shed?

Though you and Mr. Corrigan *lived intimate*
your heart was not for love
but for giving clothes to East End kids,
Parisian lingerie
to your mother's oldest friend, and money
to send a hapless nephew on to school.

You must have known your guests went home
and, in their diaries,
recorded what you said: *L'Apres-midi
du'n Faune? What do I want
with a ballet about a telephone?* Or
*No, I never saw the Dardanelles
but I had a letter of introduction to them.*
People laughed behind your back,
their gossip telling more
about themselves than you. War came.

You were in France, money frozen in New York.
So Göring got your emerald, Hitler
your gold dressing case. You used
the funds against them to pass out cigarettes
and bread to soldiers, give away felt slippers
for ulcerated feet. I sit

with my own vanity reminded how I, too,
dream myself a place in history.
I might have grown to love you
as so many did. I might
have giggled in my soup. I see you
in furs, with your surgically widened eyes
staring from the page. Though
you never could completely close those lids
in sleep, you're winking now—keeping
your secret—certain that wig will never slip.

PROMISES

Mama, humming a kind of paradise-tune
as she measured our new house
for curtains, wore the yellow shape
of a lantern in the window.
In the dim shed at the end of the garden,
was a blue enamel bowl of earth
which I lifted
to empty by the straggling forsythia.
But the dirt was hard
and full of soft, ugly stones
which Mama called *bulbs*. She laughed,
promising someday they'd flower
multicolored as my skirts in air.

That graveyard we walked stiffly past
each Sunday was green, dark
and cool. It made me quiet.
In heavy summer I'd sit there
with my book, take off my shoes
and brushing feet or fingers
against the moss I'd think *God's velvet*
and wish I could dress up in it.
I'd touch the lichen on tilted stones.
Rough as Papa's chin, it looked
like something growing on the moon.

The years we lived that end of town
I was happiest beneath that vast
oak, its shade sifting
above several small graves
blanked by leaves and lichen.
The bulbs I'd found lined
our flagstone walk, crocus
and blue hyacinth returning to surprise me
every spring. A few days

before I was sent away to school,
Papa found me beneath my tree. I sat
with book closed, humming, my left
forefinger moving back and forth
against a stone like I was spreading
lotion on a bruise. His face
paled to nothing, then he told me
of you, my twin, the mirror
buried below my drifting hand.

From that day I've felt wrenched
from a world where flowers
grow deceptively from stone.
I move from place to place
circling in return
to that bone of self I once slept next to.

for Dickie Chopping

ON TRANSLATION

The man, who scrubs,
wipes out the ashtrays one by one
but his wife's
half-filled cup of water
remains smudged
beside her incessant pile of books.

In the passage, a photograph of their child
grins like a candle on this windy night.
The severe white paint
bears no fingerprints.

What accuracies!
The moon drags the harbor deeper and deeper.
They have lived together in such a way
they are beyond wounding one another.

Something, which waits, is always telling lies.

After men and metal broke her dusty skin
the moon had to practice rising again, get back
in balance. I've heard
this is what confused the earth and the small
electric spirits our bodies hold.

There are men who remember one thing
or another about their mothers. They want
to drag me into darkness. There are children
who smash the bones of strangers until the sky
runs milky and wind stops. Down,

down beneath water and stone, the earth
cracks open and must be filled again
by pulling us back toward a nest of fire.
On these ordinary nights and days, we stumble
to rip off a page, break a vase, a head, a heart.

The red autumn berries I touched in childhood
are no longer cheerful. They haunt
the leafy soft floor of that forest by the sea.
Fog slips in and stays so I lose my face
and am afraid of what shifts behind me.

To wake each day to this and still reach
toward another living skin
is a dangerous miracle. Each day's the last,
an everlasting which treads the hinge of mystery
like a determined spider on mirror's edge.

The hour of the seventh wave splits against rock
where something, done with waiting, rises.

TWO

WRONG WEATHER

Words parch and crowd
at their edges. Flowers
pale. There is too
much light. I need rain.
This wide sun
confuses children.
The sandman won't come
until late, and not
happily. Comfort burns
away. The sea glitters—
not with dancing
or bounty, but keeping
its true fish far
beneath a secret collapse
of ice which,
intriguing the sun's
eye, shines.

ON THE OUTER BANKS

In the silver ballast of their Airstream,
Fredus M. Berger & his "missus" fried up
salmon patties made of pink shreds from a tin.
They had a thin schoolroom taste
in the violet seaside dusk.
Our tent, pitched nearby on sand, stood tilted
& adolescent compared to the Berger's
provisions & folding chairs. A yellow lamp
sizzled bugs away from our just-
getting-acquainted-talk. The next day
I watched you & Fredus fishing in the surf.
The sun, the sky, all the sea & shore curved
in a huge white blank & for the first
time ever I collapsed from heat, became
the indolent depletion of falling absolutely down:
a strangle of hair at my neck,
the running streams of my arms & legs,
those distant knees & toes. Forced
by such enormous brightness to just let go,
I touched a further shimmering world
which roared like the engine of the sun.
For a moment I slept at its center.
Somehow salvaged, I came to as Mrs. Berger
poured iced tea. Later that year
I stopped loving you. The walls closed in. Still,
I praised the grey-haired Bergers, back
in Tennessee, with their opened tins
of fish & baby peas. That bright hunk of metal
anchored in their yard had ruffled curtains
& plastic figurines. But its stories of travel
continued to gleam in the shadow of that house
where one old man & his wife
curled into each other without question, or fear.

MODESTY

How attentive are the churchyard trees.
Meticulously, they turn
and return the air. Caught up
in their *brio*
she remembers a certain man's eyes were petals
on water. He has
an inner wrist she intends to touch with her thumb.

She can't tell him of this. The mind's
no use. She requires some kind of singing,
strong as lilac. Or the sea.

One day she'll lift herself like a spoon towards his tasting
and croon of a fallen sparrow arched on stone.
Its one perfect eye
still stares brightly at passing feet.
A factual eye that forgives.

The moon was crescent and low
the last time she saw him. This man
has no idea how she's stitched
and unstitched her mouth defenselessly for years.
He doesn't know
of the sparrow's snapped off song.

She admits he is simply someone she noticed
who then spoke to her, that any word
may equal a melody that stuns.
Alone in her hour of extensive tropical blue,
she stretches all the way out of today's body, out
of immortality.

MY OTHER INSOMNIA

It's early, so dark. Wind spatters & slams. All I am
is tiredness, a punch-blue-drunk interior as the clock
ticks toward light on this rain-wild, almost day.

To place like firewood or coal a head, arms, feet or hand—
with the blood-cream of eye smeared across it—into a basket
for burning, has me refuse this world, choose *nest* & nobody else.

My first boyfriend was Armenian, from Brooklyn & safely named John.
He wore black, creased Chinos & a turquoise shirt
beside the volleyball net that camptime summer. Distinct

in the firefly dusk, he shone like pondwater
& polished stones. His syllables cracked to the side. Cornered
by the vanity of bitten nails & tomboy hair, *Armenian*

meant nothing, except it wasn't me. A word silky as rain sliding
down the window, or a new food filling my mouth. But yesterday's torn
wool, bloodied snow, pock of bullets on wall & bone make me

want to hide, or sleep. What do I really *know* in this violent dawn
where rooms stay warm if the bills are paid? I'm safe, useless
against those drenched & foreign blades. So, I remember John

& our soft, misplaced kisses as I hear the thick
blue rain outside batter to get in & fill my sleeplessness
with that cold, other burning from which I'm not immune.

January, 1990

THE ELVIS WALL

Walking that high jagged border
between Graceland and the rest of the world,
I read those tender declarations
of desire addressed to the afterlife.
So touched I cannot see where the highway
weeps down toward Mississippi, I think
romance is a made place—

It's that forest where a boy's face
beneath the moon glows white,
tinged with blue. The wind
in leafless branches is why
he folds his coat around a girl.
She, leaning on his shoulder, recalls
a story where a man once kissed
a woman's palm, closed her fingers over
so she could pocket his love
before the train pulled out. Those two,
huddled against prowling wind, close in
on that erotic fictive moment
when a famous lover
first sights the violet sprig of vein
marking his beloved's inner elbow . . .

Grinning in the sun in Memphis on an April
afternoon, I read every single word
written on stone while the hill
of lawn beyond lifts toward that froth-
white mansion hovering
like holiness
in an illustated Bible.

OUR SOLITUDES

Instead of my city window
with its humid gaze and bitten leaves,
I request a boat and that moment
when a man rests at the gunwale as the sea's
glass-green hand accepts the fact of him.

The small far shore has widened
so all at once his eyes sweep across each place
he took his girl: churchyard, quarry,
field. His girl was nothing like
this evening's passionless sea.

To the left of the quay, uphill,
is the house where she moves about
in her dull kitchen, its yellow ribbon
of light slipping at her hands.
She's gathered up the supper things.

Her passion is not for such things
but for the damp mud which streaked her knees
as her mouth fell across him
in a starlit field. The boat steams in
but no moon rises above our personal harbor.

My window shuts on this moonless night.
The woman's mouth tightens
as the man walks home away from her.
Cool air borders the doorway where she stands
while desire settles for starker mysteries.

Still, we request a specific sea
where flecked salt air arouses.

TO S. KAZUKO

That wintery afternoon you called me up
and asked for company, your thin
exotic voice crumpled with unhappiness.
But I was newly in love. He stood
there in my kitchen with his cigarettes
and whisky, his hawk-edged eyes
dismissive of anything but his own talk.
So I said I couldn't meet you then,
turned right back to him and stayed
for several years. Because
the marriage crazed and you were Japanese,
lonely beneath Iowa's bitter flat sky,
I've never forgotten. I'm sorry now
for that vacancy in your drab
extensive day, for giving nothing back
when you'd enchanted me
with stories of jazz club life,
and what you'd worn those nights
you went out dancing with Mishima Yukio.

LACE CURTAINS

Hunched in her green silk blouse and pearls,
she's flat out drunk by noon.
Upstairs, her two small children
grumble the wheels of a wooden truck
across the playroom floor.
In the kitchen, Nanny spoons tinned soup for lunch.
The harbor blurs in summer sun, dusty
hydrangeas barely stir.

This young wife feels nothing
but a faint blame that what exists around her
is not what she wished. Above the mantle,
that painting of a white horse in a field
windows another world
with its cool hint of birdsong and running streams.

There's no sound from the children
as they dress for the beach. The back door closes.
The woman shakes free her hair, then stumbles
across the room up
to where the horse stares out at her.
The meadow bristles lightly with red flowers.
Leaning to hear some bird call, she presses
her palms hard against just one
of four walls.

AT THE HIGH-WATER MARK

I pluck a gull's breastbone away from feathers and weed.
Poor bird, brought in by water—
its white cartilage has the shape of a mouth
open for inspiration, or flight.

I watch the white glaze of bad weather cool against the sky
like a cheap underslip through which shines
the sun's eye, briefly. I've never liked this dead
height of summer which presses at windows with its long hours.

There's a man not far from here whose blindness
is pale as daytime fog. At least he's not
a child caught in darkness beneath the stairs.
His life is courageous, his bright bandage almost heavenly.

Perhaps that gull slammed first into the sun before it broke apart
leaving something for my fingers to snap off in sand.
The glare from water, that slide of air nagging
at my eyes, makes my body falter.

This wishbone in my hand is as light as the almost-
nothing of a prayer.

GOOD FRIDAY

The city readies itself for Easter hymns
and cocaine. Leaves flail
in unseasonable wind and red, pink, yellow
petals scatter across indifferent lawns
on this day I no longer love you.

There was a woman I knew who broke her body
into the sea. Her blood swiftly left
the shoreline and took on the no-color of wind.
Once she'd been a flower, a bride
who capped her long dark hair with a veil
and smiled for a man.
Inside, she was very serious and looked away.

I remember how she laughed and smoked,
the cold slippery bottles of milk
in the crook of her arm as she swung herself
up the street each morning. She is why, now,

in a city far away I say no to myself
as I think of you and those terrible words
you'd cry: "What are we going to do! What,
what shall we do?" I think of how that woman
answered herself, and how it felt
when I refused to answer you.

The air is bright today. A calico cat
crouches on the sill while birds
inhabit the sudden gusts above their nests
and my blood calms. I want forgiveness
and speak my gratitude for small
easeful things: coffee, phone calls, sauce
on the stove. The precision
of my existence no longer touches you.

For all the living, I pray that "What
shall we do?" be lifted away

as our blood and bodies begin to revive—
when no longer loving
is to love again, and survive.

MELANCHOLIA

In the amber shadow-and-sway of the oil lamp
she is less than beautiful
as she leans forward biting her lip,
scratching her knee.
Because he has not told her the truth
exactly, he makes his fingers
skim up and down her back, then turns
to kiss her shoulder.
For some minutes he feels ashamed.

Through the half-shut window, a smell
of overripe apples drifts from crates
piled in the street.
He blows out the lamp but, unlike her,
does not sleep. He imagines
gently holding a nettle against her cheek.

FIGURE & GROUND

(after looking at some pictures by Francis Bacon)

I like to touch fire, thread
myself to flicker & surge.
Despite shape-shifting
& its enemy greed, fire
pleasures my existence.

One dusky hour on a hill
looking out across a violet sea,
I leaned against a stone
to watch the sky flare & knew
I'd been caught between heart & eye.

Someone I loved was with me,
a potion of wind rushing
at my mouth. Though he still
shifts across my dreams,
I don't mind. In a world

with so many torn shirts, exploded
faces, mouths struck open
for screaming, he's not
much trouble. Those bright
mouths streaked yellow, red

& green splash wide as any sky
above the burnished sea. Desire's
such a little thing on the surface
of this earth where we live
already catching fire.

THE QUESTION OF NOON

No stares itself in the face, a word
made two ways at once.
Compared to that, the four winds
are simple. They rise
and leave like breath, returning

so we may step in further directions.
But we don't. The world
is lived two ways at once, two ways
and more. Noon
points back to the center of night

when those who sleep
are untroubled unless they dream.
We're all a matter of love
and blood, the love for blood
flowering on stone as our eyes widen

in terror and relief. Noon—
when we lay our tables to feed
while woodland animals avoid us
in thickets and caves, when fish glide
to the deepest possible waters.

How does no turn into yes, become
a gesture which lavenders the sheets
or kisses a child's scraped knee?
Perhaps it's just a listening
so God, or someone else, may join us.

A moment of noon. Suddenly
sun sweeps through the window lighting a face
which is waiting out this war.
There's still a terrible noise
in the streets and wind

rises against the battered garden.
Who can live like this
among torn flowers? Who will wash
these stones which have been washed
so many times before?

NAIVE READING

Walking back from town, I kick aside
a dry chicken bone which cracks
light as a leaf. Later, I read that in the street
outside your window is the ghost
of a dead policeman and wonder
which is lighter, ghost or leaf?
By the constable's side a child, Eileen,
tugs at his torn green cuff.
She clutches a splayed cloth doll.

On the broken pavement, a scattering
of sparrows and blood softens
in the pin-prick fog. In your world
fog and murder keep returning.
They remind you how once, at school,
a boy opened his kerchief to reveal
six fledglings he'd smashed with an ax.
Looking up taught you forever
what God allows on a human face.

Here, an ocean away, the sweet
tang of magnolias drifts among children
playing on this ordinary afternoon.
Only mockingbirds and crows attack the lawns
to feed. My eyes grow tired. I lean
above the sink to splash what skin
still covers bone. I'm in the mirror
not yet taking sides. But behind me
something stirs light as summer leaves

or an eyelash of God—your ghosts
that lick across the world, like fog.

ON A DRAB DECEMBER HILL

On a drab December hill, a handful of men
spread out with their dogs, clappers and guns.
They look like figures from a picture book,
or film, so I open my window to watch.

Some birds make it, uprushing the air
to glide out over the glen. Some
stall, plummet where dogs arrive.
My stomach knots—

the way a child feels curled in the dark
listening to parents quarrel.
Like her, I'm racked by the long
grey silences between. Out on the path

a muddy Jack Russell, nose to the ground,
trots like a wind-up toy. The child
wraps a pillow around her head and hums
till her skull buzzes with a soft, blank noise.

AUTUMN IS A PLACE

(at the Barbara Hepworth Museum)

Autumn is a place in the heart where Orion is back in season.
In the famous garden, the sculptor's white bed
in its white-washed shed, still suggests her shape: an oval
carved for holding water, or a child. Sometimes,
on difficult nights, she'd lie down, shift
out of pain and float up over bronze, stone and thick
flowering trees past the roofs of Barnoon
into a fresh northerly sky.
Like any angel, her cramped fingers straightened, legs
kicked free to dance as she hammered at the stars—
their gestures of a molten heart enfolding
one heaven, one earth.

I walk this garden often where the flesh of stone and bronze,
the ligaments of stems and string form a single
body of place in the mind. Today I step against a bee
who searches the wrong, late air for pollen. I watch
a spider suspended between quince-branch and white
falling flowers. She tries clutching two flies at once.
How quickly our bodies call us away from what we do
and love. Our hands, elbows, shoulders, legs become confused
as the shape of things scatters and breaks
like autumn's torn sounds cracking.
In the workshop

Dame Barbara's smock still hangs, tools tilt and dust
won't quite settle. Three white spheres wait for incision
while huge marble blocks shrug, then sigh back down towards dirt.
It was the nature of stone to be pleased by her. It's the nature
of her garden to thicken with leaves, for wind to snap
and stream beneath a grainy sky. In her shed, the white chenille
spread wears a water-stain but the pillow's plumped just right.
A churchbell tolls. Bronze and stone hold still. I walk
the whole chilled circle of garden returning to fallen

petals and that spider
just reaching for a last black speck in her web.

Our local angel

knows of pain and fire. She spreads her wings, opens her hands
in blessing. Stone and bronze release their breath and warm
air rises across all our gardens and lost bodies
until pain smooths out beneath St. Ia's mackerel skies.
In the studio, dust settles for today. The spider sleeps.

In memory of Harry T. Kuenzel, 1943-1990

THREE

DOMESTICS

This day holds grey and still. Rain begins
as an ambulance, with its urgent tenor,
stops along the road. We watch, with small guilt,
from the attic window until it drives away
followed by the doctor's car. A local death,
anonymous until the card's displayed. Twenty years

and an ocean away, another *we* watched the quick
medics and police screeching through the winter dark
of Baltimore. From just across the street
we'd heard the shot, a scream, the woman kill
what came at her with a knife. We watched her plead
her story to the cops until they dragged her off,

handcuffed since she was black. She staggered in a heavy
khaki coat, head bowed, hopeless. I recall my shock
while sitting with my book on a dull green sofa
to hear the real sound of murder. I remember
upturned faces, and the red-white slashing lights.
Often I've wondered what became of her in that unkind,

nearly southern city. She'd have had to wait,
months at least, downtown in a creased denim dress
with rationed cigarettes and one streaked toilet
shared with strangers in the corner of that cell. March,
April, May: outside magnolias lifting their blossoms
toward sky, dogwood spattering the yards, great ships

hauling in and out of harbor. Inside, an anxious woman
and one brown coat, one purse, abandoned to a dusty locker.
It's hard to watch such things, to remember. It's
harder not to, as though we could clutch tight the secret
of getting through a day by watching others
not make it. Heavy weather drags the stain

across us. Tomorrow, it's ten years
since Sheila died, shot not once but four times

by her husband. This morning
I'd been sitting with another book only a little
less in the dark than all those years ago.
Some things bruise forever.

THE MEADOW

The man with a thick black beard is picture-
framed by sky and trees. His shirt is blue.
Sleeves rolled, he bends into tall feathery grasses,
fingers choosing a shimmer of flowers
as part of the ritual for his child. That's how
the daughter must invent this man who never
sang, or brushed back her hair on any feverish night.
It doesn't matter. The meadow shines. Yellow, white,
orange and blue wildflowers fleck the surface of its world.
The bouquet trembles. The story of its gathering
began the moment that her father shut the door
behind him and vanished towards another life.
She never saw his eyes. As she grew
she chose his face and open arms as though absence
were not her fault, or even his. Years
and years now—the texture of objects, the damp
skin of husbands, the shifting colors of all cats
who've ever needed her have proved the father
will not come back. Still, a child in red sweater
and shoes keeps running towards that figure
crouched and bearded in tall grass. He lifts
his arms, beckons and she steps high, again
and again delighted, as long as the meadow lasts.

FICTION'S DAUGHTER

I eat myself a family: each quart of ice cream, a tidy
blonde Mom in shirtwaist and pearls crossing the lawn
with a pitcher of fresh lemonade. When she bakes
my whole house smells like paradise. I dream each slab
of chocolate is a perfect Dad in thin important suits
calling "Honey, I'm home!" at 5:25 p.m. precisely.
Me and Little Sister (whose name I can't decide) tumble
into his hugs. My sister likes for me to brush
her hair, weave ribbons through her toes. She's
those boxes of crackers I consume, brisk and gold.

For Christmas I eat cookies and hunks of cheese until my red
velvet stocking hangs beside a *real* fire and I hear
a world full of chimes, not the constant clack of typing.
You'd think knowing all this I could stop,
but I'm someone else's story. My dark, word-
drunk father hardly eats at all.
He looms right into his books and papers,
then later gently blows a goodnight kiss.
But I'm not safe for sleep unless I *know* I'm tall,
gorgeous, and thin! Sure,

I have the right long bones, am dusky and pretty
like my first mother. I wear her fire and the red mouth
of her wine-stained lips. But she left, and I am left
wide-hipped, built too big for any love to hold.
My first protection is the finger down my throat. Two
step-mothers later, there's less of me. I'd hoped those Moms
would dress for dinner, fuss prettily about a pretty house.
I'd hoped we'd all sit down together. I still long for
that white canopy-bed I saw in a picture when I was five.
I hate boring rooms where only books, and Dad, remain the same.

Those bad-girl nights when biscuits break up in my hands,
I hear the sound of Little Sister's feet brushing
beside me on the way to school. I can't stop
filling myself with my t.v. dreams of family. I'm told

I'm self-destructive—what do they expect—these artists
who made me wrong? With each wrench, each stomach heave
and lash of sweat I try to start again, twist back to zero.
One night I'll float downstairs into the warm
red arms of Santa Claus, into a home where nothing's
criminal and my whole body fills with inhabitant love.

THE CANOE IN THE FOREST

Like a sliver of light adrift in the pine & russet shade
the canoe in the forest
has moved down to the riverbank, into the slow thick
water of a late August afternoon. Or you could say
that my grandfather with his wolf-
haired hands shifted the heavy tarp
& with a few slick tugs that silver eyelid of a boat
slid out, trembling
in the shallows as he stepped in.

I saw him, barechested, whiskered & red, slam the door,
stride away. I pictured that blonde
paddle dipping—stroke, feather, stroke—downstream
until he was as solitary as he wished to be.
Back in the cool house, the air
relaxed. People did as they pleased. The next day

felt thick with the smoke of many cigarettes.
I was barely spoken to until
I-don't-remember-who sat me down & said *Grandpa*
found a dead man in the river. Grandpa touched him
with his canoe. For months, I squinted from that river's shine,
cast my eyes about for the gone-to-sleep-shape
of a man in water. I looked by trees, trashcans,
in the lavatory at school—sure
I'd step around some simple corner & there he'd be.

Still, all canoes with their silvers, reds & greens
keep slipping along rivers, & dark New England lakes.
How beautiful
the paddle's dip & swing, the merest scrape
of water side to side. How time & light adore those surfaces
of motion, the touch of
one canoe sliding into that celestial chill
which grazed my Grandpa's cheek at the same
moment as water
held, & mirror-cold metal went bump.

DOGS

Whose roses are being torn apart
by wind and black abrasive rains?
They fall together, thorns
piercing petals and stems
as though a herd of schoolgirls
had maddened in a sewing room
threading thumb to cheek,
torso to thigh. Little girls
caught by wind's heedless desire
slashing across the lawn.

Another little girl walks to the store with
two nickles and a dime. Coming home, she stops
to poke hello at the wrong dog. He sinks
his teeth hard into her hand. Her mother panics.
No policeman can find this dog. After yelling,
the mother lets the child put iodine on the hand
herself. It colors to rust. Her tears hurt too,
but going to the doctor is a big white blank.
Something with eyes from the ceiling watches as
they hold the child down and needles ease into
her smooth white abdomen. Something watches
like a big window or a piece of fire falling
across her.

The slightest shift of stone,
the smallest sound, prepare
catastrophe for two
speckled eggs resting on the sill.
No bird comes to claim them.

She remembers the little plaid jacket she wore,
and the few streaks of blood she carried home.
She feels her sticky rusted fingers, and the
policeman's breath close to her face. The rest

is impossible except for black winds, the cross-
hatched rain, a needle's eye? Her mother's open mouth.

Some evenings, God stays
in the sunset above the field
and trees. He plays
the two-pronged song of the phoebe,
or shades that painting
of blue deer leaping a canyon
pinned above her bed. Sometimes
He's Mother humming in the bath.

But who fills up the night
with those black dogs
lifting her hand away
between their teeth? That hand,
and the rest of her, pulled
into thickets or deep
below the dark brown pond
where lily pads
float above her head?

On the lawn, those roses
stay undone—yellow and pink
flattened in mud, thorns
gone soft, leaves
curled up—all flung down
like dresses after a dance.

Little stones in the stream nearby
get pushed from their shallow nests
by tawny rushed waters.
Twilight falls thin as silk
above the phoebe and a sudden
thrush. The field beyond
seeps toward the last gleam

from birches where a doe
steps out to graze. God sleeps
in two eggs on the sill
where the child leans on her elbows
to stare into that ceiling-sky
which is not blank
but punctured by stars. Poor big sky
chewed rough at the edges by branches
and leaves. A voice calls
from the bottom of the stairs.
Dreams click awake
testing their teeth on the rafters.

INFREQUENT MYSTERIES

1.

My baffled soul, you're still scanning that list of names
for the right angel to talk to,
still searching the kindly shelter of the blossoming
apple tree which once spread wings
in the lower orchard, still
seeking that blue silk dress of childhood swinging
its hem above party shoes.
You can't take no for an answer, you won't
recognize yes.

My silly hands that make mistakes, my eyes
that alight in the wrong places and spend time there
thinking "that's what I want!"—
What next, my tough spreading feet, my knees
the color of mottled moons?

And arrogant heart, all gnarled and sighing,
don't you know none of them exist? Father
is not there, the lover is not there, Grandmother
is leaving. And what of the children?
Those words "you thought less of the little girl"
were told you in a dream. . . .

None of them exist.
I want to pin up my hair in a final farewell
and turn to the sea, or the church tower, for reassurance.
I promise I will call my friend in another town
and ask for his help. I will attempt to visit
the old lady.
And then will you forgive me? You who don't exist?

2.

If I kiss you, my life will stop.
So the world comes to take my mouth away.

I must tell you I had a sign
the way, at four years of age, I had chicken pox
in a darkened room. Its refuge
to curl against my grandmother—rocking, rocking.

I wear its mark on my face. I wear this sign
like my thickened ankle I broke when I was drunk.

If I kiss you hard the world as I know it
will stop. Just think—
I may not like it. You may not like it.

So the world would stop, and then go on.

3.

This morning I watch the sea
the way anyone watches the sea from shore.
I try to open myself
away from fear, let the world
remove my voice.

Aware of a flight of sparrows above tall grass,
I find I like my prepositions.
They place me where I am—here—alive
beside the cries of children
at water's edge, beneath
the asking-asking noise of gulls,
not far from where a bee
scolds clover for moving in the wind.

This moment, I blame no one for anything
because your face, looking down at me
from a dream, bore the vast
expression of the sky and told me
blame was useless. This moment

the sea enjoys itself and the sky
is simply everywhere above the world.

4.

The man, who was a father, curls against the bedclothes.
He strokes the strap of a watch
for protection, a watch borrowed from the wife
of a dead man. His wide eyes shrug back
from the doorway where his son stands uncertain of words,
of who he sees. The window beyond

stares out at hydrangeas and distressed
summer roses blowing apart in a grey wind.
Inside and outside it is grey. The air above the garden
whirls around, slams at the panes. But the air
above the bed, beside the wardrobe, has stopped short
like an old dog waiting for directions.

The son insists on tea for the man,
rouses him into clothes. The son
tries to shake the air to clarity. The watch,
which is digital and not ticking, looks
for language to persuade: "Get up, go on,
turn toward your flowers which need you."

5. *Storybook*

The town has fallen through a hole in the lake.
On the bank stand a man and his donkey
staring down through the torn water.
The roofs, steeples, pavements and trees
all keep gliding away. The man
and the donkey blame each other
because all their food, all their friends
have fallen through. But the lake

is lit golden in the late afternoon.
Deceptive gold around a beautiful watery throat.
The pines on the ridge go almost black.
It's a long journey into them to the dark
center where fires blaze at the same moment
a seam closes in the lake. The man and the donkey
are left, bewildered, gazing
at the torn pages of their love.

6.

There's a time before anything is sure—
Is birdsong bright
or dark, have stones on the beach
been lifted for a reason?

These are pieces of a world I don't inhabit
so I watch the sea, heavy
with moon, rushing at me to say
how dare I contain it with words!

It snorts like many horses all at once,
cares less that I walk
on that silver stain of sand where clouds
reflect their salmon-pink
this certain morning before storms come.

*

There are walls, small spaces, and walls
which we call something else. Television wall,
books, a lover across town.
That change of name between one moment of the self
and another. Most talking is a wall,
certainly the daily phrase. The personal
is a small space, or no space at all
until something calls from the world outside.

*

I hear the sound of rain before it falls, see
the light-coming-down which becomes
that sound. How inexact I am
among the people within these walls.
Rain comes from a world outside.

This moment I live in the wall
of my skull where it's raining.
I want only the dark sound of it—
that thin pure voice to inhabit me.

7.

I want to go out, so it can take me in.
Not fire, earth, water—but air—
my answerable twin.

Let it come into this house which is ready
to blow apart! The wind outside
rattles like that first knowledge
of another person. Inside,
language is just a mouse in the skirtingboards.
Let it come in like a judge
or possible friend. Don't let me fall
through the burning windows.

I'm just a moment in this room
adrift among syllables. My prayers
fall like desire, or flags of rain over the sea.
Notice, the door's unlocked
as for Elijah. I'm ready to lift my face.

THE CRICKETS OF AMHERST

On the downhill slope of this yard, a flock
of irises—white, purple, yellow, blue—
dim and sway beneath the evening star.
The crickets, hidden and soothing,
weave a timeless quaver in the air
around this large white house where children
settle after supper
and grown-ups murmur in the yellow kitchen.

I lie alone on damp grass.
Only the distant grumble of traffic
defines which century I drift slowly through.
The flowers, with their dipped
darkening heads, are suddenly women grieving.
Crickets become the thin
blue whistle of boys returning from the war
down South. Churchbells toll. Still,

bread proves on shelves above the fire.
A white dress smooths out
in its lavender-spiced wardrobe and a small girl
drops the last jar of brandied peaches
to a scatter of harvest moons on cellar stairs.
One man leans his crutch against a wall
and sits down in the pure room of home.
His mother's hand just dares to touch his shoulder.

A churchbell tolls, pitches higher to the *now-now*
of a siren slicing past the famous college.
Crickets chitter and lilt.
Indoors, another child is dreaming
and through the window I hear that thrash of war
he enters as he sleeps. Grown-ups
raise their voices above radio-song.
The man curses. Crickets stop.
A rash of fireflies sprinkles the dark
as though just tipped through a crack in heaven's jar.

NOTES

"Occultations":
Paintings by Steve Dove, The Salt House Gallery, St. Ives, Cornwall.

"Lesson of the Day":
I am indebted to Brian Masters' *Great Hostesses*.

"At the High-Water Mark":
The "man not far from here" is the astonishing Cornish poet, Jack Clemo.

"Naive Reading":
A response to Jack Holland's *Too Long a Sacrifice*.

"Autumn is a Place":
While the poem was written in St. Ives, it's given now to Harry Kuenzel who was a most remarkable craftsman and the best sort of human being. For many many people near where I live, there's no doubt he is a beloved, local angel.

My especial gratitude to the Hawthornden Castle International Writers' Retreat where so many of these poems first took shape, and thanks for their care and attention to John Barnie, Patricia Bishop, Cynthia Hogue, Stella Johnston, Alistair MacNaughton, Sharon Mayberry, Sandy Solomon and Dana Weimer. Also thanks to Nigel James for all the energy and clear-talking and particular thanks to E.B. for helping me to re-focus.

POETRY FROM ALICE JAMES BOOKS